C000099565

CONTENTS

© Copyright 2019 by Joseph Sorensen

All rights reserved

This document is geared towards providing exact and reliable information with regard to the topic and issue covered. The publication is sold with the idea that the publisher is not required to render accounting, officially permitted, or otherwise, qualified services. If advice is necessary, legal or professional, a practiced individual in the profession should be ordered.

From a Declaration of Principles which was accepted and approved equally by a Committee of the American Bar Association and a Committee of Publishers and Associations.

In no way is it legal to reproduce, duplicate, or transmit any part of this document in either electronic means or in printed format. Recording of this publication is strictly prohibited and any storage of this document is not allowed unless with written permission from the publisher. All rights reserved.

The information provided herein is stated to be truthful and consistent, in that any liability, in terms of inattention or otherwise, by any usage or abuse of any policies, processes, or directions contained within is the solitary and utter responsibility of the recipient reader. Under no circumstances will any legal responsibility or blame be held against the publisher for any reparation, damages, or monetary loss due to the information herein, either directly or indirectly.

Respective authors own all copyrights not held by the publisher.

The information herein is offered for informational purposes solely, and is universal as so. The presentation of the information is without contract or any type of guarantee assurance.

The trademarks that are used are without any consent, and the publication of the trademark is without permission or backing by the trademark owner. All trademarks and brands within this book are for clarifying purposes only and are the owned by the owners themselves, not affiliated with this document.

DISCLAIMER

All erudition contained in this book is given for informational and educational purposes only. The author is not in any way accountable for any results or outcomes that emanate from using this material. Constructive attempts have been made to provide information that is both accurate and effective, but the author is not bound for the accuracy or use/misuse of this information.

INTRODUCTION

Bulimia nervosa, as well simply known as bulimia, is conceived as an eating disorder characterized by binge eating followed by purging. The pathology of BN mirrors the structure of the self conveyed sensory system, which makes patients feeling self inadequacy.

Commonly known and treated as binge eating, it refers to eating a huge amount of aliments in a short length of time. Usually, patients affected by this illness tend to get rid of the food consumed, this practice may be done by taking laxatives or vomiting, it has been recorded as well that the use of stimulants such as water, diuretics or extreme exercise is a common practice.

The Main issue regarding a patient caught binge eating is the concept of being a pig together with cheating on a mental rule self-imposed involving a food plan that doesn't stick anymore. This self victim usually undermines a lack of confidence in the ability of self-control.

Learning how to recognize and ignore this internal sense is the first step on how to finally stop binge eating. In the following chapter, several tips will be discussed on how to understand and prevent food addictions.

There is a distinction between obsessive over-alimentation and bulimia nervosa. Persons who binge and suffer from bulimia will undertake activities that help their bodies to get rid of the food they have recently consumed. However, people coping with excessive compulsive eating do not indulge in such behavior.

Signs And Symptoms

BN usually involves a rapid and out of control eating disorder, it may calm down at the moment when the binge eater is stopped by another member of the family or friends, this phenomenon can as well stop itself following pain in the stomach because of overextension, which typically causes vomiting or purging.

Binge eating can represent itself several times in a week or days in a raw during a month, causing unfortunately, gastric reflux, dehydration, electrolyte, Boerhaave syndrome and in the worst-case oral traumas.

Biologically speaking there is scientific evidence that this disorder may be held in genetics such as abnormal levels of hormones like serotonin, responsible for the most common eating disorders.

There are several different explanations of why you may be overeating, and generally, they are all caused by events in your life. It could be work-related and frustrating, or it could be a more personal problem like your self-esteem, your self-perception, or the level of gladness that is the critical cause.

Here is a list of the most popular reasons that you have to eat and helpful tips so you can start taking a healthier diet that will enhance your health and help you regulate your eating habits

1. Being bored

2. Low self-confidence

3. Overwhelmed Or Of Worked

4. Being Upset Or Disappointment

5. A Medical Condition

If you have a food problem, try to evaluate the situation and find out what the best solutions will be for you. The key is to find the trigger that causes your problem and then find a solution that suits your lifestyle so that you can stick to your question and do everything you need to combat it.

Food disorder research has gone a long way over the past 25-30 years. Professionals are now aware that stress and significant changes in lives like divorce, college movement, marriage, or a new job can all lead to binge mental illnesses. Here are five tips for beginning your recovery journey:

1. Stress Healing

Stress is the first reason we keep bingeing, seek not to surpass the timetable.

2. Avoid questioning Healing

You judge yourself because, in some or many ways, you find like you are not good enough.

3. Challenge your convictions.

Belief systems or values and beliefs that you carry are based on the ideas of others, such as your parents, mentors, religious leaders, teachers, and the society at large. Belief is really the mental condition in which an individual is persuaded of the validity of an argument. Often we recognize only the views of others without knowing whether we believe they are wrong or right as we establish beliefs from several different sources

4. Practice visualization and meditation Healing

Meditation is the process of attempting to concentrate your attention uncritically on one issue at a time. It is relatively irrelevant what it is, and differs from tradition to tradition. The meditator often repeats a syllable, group, or word of words aloud or silently. It is called mantra therapy.

5. Using optimistic phrases

Positive words are fantastic! You 're what keeps you going when you're sad or when these little voices you hear are trying to undermine your best efforts. You can use positive statements combined with an enthusiastic feeling to achieve what you really want in your mind. You should write your own optimistic words to accomplish your goals. Write it on a piece of paper ten or twenty times, and tell them loudly, with enthusiasm and joy. Do this for a few days, then pick another statement you want to use. When you say your comments loudly, you believe what you say is valid. Affirmations that are regularly used become part of the belief system and often produce results

Feel free to wake up every morning and greet with renewed determination this day! You may rise up and say, "Today is the day I will keep to my diet and weight loss objectives throughout the day." What a fantastic optimistic way to start your new day. The beginning of a better day, a fresh start, lies ahead of you. However, as experience has really shown, good intentions alone are sometimes not enough to overcome the craving for food. Alone, willpower is not enough to overcome the desire for eating, binging, or overdriving comfort. The positive intention must be related to a concrete action plan. A predetermined, personalized action plan provides empowerment. You want an original idea, which you think carefully in advance and write down.

Think about it-when was your last 'fast' binge or craved sidestepped? Otherwise, you went through the fast-food restaurant effortlessly when you felt stressed, fatigued, depressed, or bored? Your urge to eat was likely so strong that it blocked all rational, objective-oriented thinking. At a time of crisis, willpower and optimism seem to be gone.

Believe this or not, there still are some of you who woke up today and said firmly that today would be a success. Some of you still want to do it without overeating throughout the day. The aspect of you hidden behind your enormous urge to eat is so confident earlier. It will be your job to find it and bring it back into the limelight. You will need some tools in your toolbox for this.

When you're in the middle of a disaster, there is no time to find new items. Instead, it is time to prepare for excellent and optimistic times. This way, they 're already there when you need them. You just have to open the box and dig it out if necessary. Use the following guidelines to organize your individual action plan to avoid any kind of craving or binge.

Planning for pre-binge

When you're in a crisis, this is often extremely difficult to see objectively what is happening. Overwhelmed by a need to feed, the insight required to look for other acts is difficult to obtain. Eating is probably your usual way to cope with what happens, so the desire can be substantial. If you are so keen to eat and to deal with the little picture of what is happening in your world, your mind will not be focused enough to recall you are great plans. What you have is a written plan that helps you to get out of the short-term problem and eating habits and into your long-term personal goals.

A. Collection of crisis approaches

To get over the need to eat, create a number of stuff you can do or have done previously. When a crisis occurs, you will determine what category or category of ideas can support you. Include suggestions in both fields as follows:

Strategies for diversion

Ideas that put fun and food away. Examples can include hobbies for painting, house cleaning, cycling, garden cultivation, etc.

Comportement Methods

Tools to help you handle your climate. Such techniques may include drinking water to see when you were really thirsty, throwing away the delicious food, inviting a mate, etc.

Self-relaxation and the techniques for comfort

What other ways can you ease your mind, body, and soul, instead of using food to calm or to feel good? For example, fragrant bath, yoga, warm, peaceful music, deep breathing, and watching the wind in the park.

Strategies for emotional needs

Consider creative ways to first recognize and then deal with the underlying emotion. Speak with a relative or lawyer, or physically sit with the newspaper. There are just a few ways to cope with anger rather than consuming it.

When your list is completed, keep it in a position that is easily accessible (e.g., refrigerator, bag, etc.) as needed. If necessary, revise or update your list.

B. List of phones

In times of crisis, it is also necessary to reach out. We every feel helpless, scared, and out of control during times of urgency. Reaching somebody during this period will help ease some of your anxiety. Often getting someone to speak to will avoid a fall or reversal. Talking to others about your thoughts will also reassure you that other people care for you and are not alone. Enter names and numbers of people who are compassionate, fully comprehend people, and feel supported. While "attaching and touching someone" may be difficult at first, it will gradually get more comfortable. The person you call will be grateful that you supported them in a rough time.

C. Mantra Personal

Develop a one or two-line statement that is important to you. Take some time with this and write a significant and robust comment in your midst. That expression is something that takes you back to the bigger picture and allows you to realize that you should take a breath and make a new decision. If a crisis occurs, read and repeat the answer before you can feel the reality inside your own body.

Begin designing your own tailored approach now. Don't worry when it's not ideal or if you don't know if the ideas you write are going to work. This is an ongoing program you are going to amend and keep tuning. In any case, no plan works. Look at your previous accomplishments and start realizing what has performed sometimes. Note also what didn't fit. Follow this simple outline and help yourself extra to avoid a binge and to produce the magnificent result you want.

Creating A Food Plan To Succeed

In this early stage, you may have examined some weight loss programs online that you spoke with your buddies about the programs with which they have succeeded or attended your local weight loss support group. You have selected, through deliberation, the strategy that seems most fitting for you. You 're excited and willing to begin. This time you know that you're going to succeed!

Take a step back before you dive in. Your chances to take these pounds off and keep them off are statistically quite dim. In one of UCLA 's most extensive studies of weight loss, while most people who follow various dietary plans lose 5-10 percent of their calorie intake, most people gain back and forth within a year.

If there are small chances of lasting success (forgive the pun), why bother? Wouldn't you hate to work so hard and then find yourself right back on the road a few months ago?

Don't fear. There is a way to trigger a permanent loss of weight. The key is to spend more time in a planning phase before you start working. Let's now create a framework for perpetual healthy eating, and you never have to start another diet again.

Prepare for Weight Loss Success

There are other beautiful tools to help you plan for a significant change. In the knowledge of fitness and wellbeing, these are seven things that can help you achieve your diet and fitness plan before beginning. Although you may be motivated to move right into your diet, it increases your chances of success by spending the effort to prepare yourself with these steps.

1. Build your own dream of wellness.

How do you think success looks like? Imagine how your life will look and sound when your weight loss target has been achieved. Don't let it depend on a scale number. What's going to be great and different? How are you going to do every day? What new diet and workout habits are you going to adopt every day? Every change of behavior leads to a change in who we are. Who are you going to be in your new healthy body trim? What are you going to be able of now you may not be?

2. Strengthen your commitment.

Writing a declaration of what you commit to will help reinforce your determination. Putting your pen into paper, taking your ideas out of your head, and agreeing in writing will help to concretize your plan. Read it aloud, or just merely to yourself, is a useful practice.

3. Growing your faith.

Regardless of your determination and encouragement, in the back of your mind, there may be a small voice whispering that you will probably fail, particularly if you have previously attempted to lose weight. Don't focus on the big picture or the number that you're trying to hit. Identify practical, tiny, and actionable steps you should take. For example, if you just miss breakfast for lunch, work to add a healthier breakfast to your day. Start three days a week (not every day perfect). If it's simple, add a fourth. Don't exercise regularly? Start a 10-minute workout like a walk a day. Through creating a plan for small, manageable changes, one step at a time, and by recognizing every success, your trust will grow.

4. Prevent barriers and develop strategies to address them.

Which weight loss barriers have you encountered in the past, or fear you will meet in the future? Predict problems before they occur and develop strategies to prevent them. Would you drive in the car for long hours and find yourself buying something to avoid starvation at road stops? Brainstorm a list of non-perishable and compact snacks.

Do your friends meet every Friday after work for a happy hour, just to drink and consume more calories than you would like? You can maybe persuade one or two of them to join you in the gym, and then go out together for a nice meal.

5. Develop a team of help.

You must understand that your duty is the task of losing weight, and there is nothing else. It doesn't mean, though, that you have to go alone. What is going to help your journey? Share your dream with friends and family and tell them how they can support you. With other people who also work on weight loss, you can swap ideas, help keep you motivated, and make your journey fun. You can also develop a team of professionals to assist you with different aspects of your weight loss journey: a physician, a doctor, a personal trainer, a new workout, or a counselor to support you in solving emotional eating issues.

6. Build a positive climate.

It's time to start talking about what wants to be in a position so that the landmines are eliminated until you take action. Are your refrigerator and your cabinets full of snacks and unpleasant choices? Give or throw it away! Give it away! Store your shelves in plenty of healthy options so that you have what you need on hand when you have hunger, or it is time to prepare dinner. It's the same for your office. Delete candy and chips from the drawers of your desk. Maintain good choices at the side. If you do not have access to a refrigerator, you might want to buy a little one or at least get more relaxed, so that you can keep the right snacks. When you intend to join a gym, please make sure your home or office is convenient. Ask for trial membership and ensure that the atmosphere is pleasant.

7. Create an action plan.

Now that the cognitive work has been done, it is time to build your plan. This is where you can decide what actions you feel like taking. Are you going to follow a formal meal plan or just slowly add nutritious food to your everyday intake? Will you start a walking program, enter a gym, or engage in a dance class at the park near your home? Do you want to begin bagging brown lunches instead of eating every day?

Don't allow your weight loss / fat loss to be discouraged by setbacks or slips and cause you to abandon! We are all wrong, so be patient and realistic about your goals and expectations. And don't forget what you face. The beauty of the program is to choose what will suit your particular life. Don't want to follow rules that you feel awkward. There is no ideal diet plan for everyone. When it comes to weight loss, one size (or diet) certainly doesn't fit everyone.

BULIMIA'S LARGE UNANSWERED INQUIRY

Signs and side effects

Symptoms and side effects of Bulimia may include:

- Gorging then vomiting practices.

- Hidden eating practices.

- Contorted impression of body shape or weight.

- Sentiments of blame and disgrace around nourishment and eating.

- Uneasiness or discouragement.

- Vanishing in the wake of eating.

- Feeling drained or dormant.

- Stomach torments.

- Steady sore throat.

- Indications of liquor abuse.

- Low confidence.

So what causes the binge to eat?

Experts are not clear about the exact causes of eating disorders in general. Yet it is widely recognized that mental wellbeing has a lot to do with it. Emotional and spiritual health factors, like depression, anxiety, bipolar disorder, or stress, certainly play a role. The genes, psychology, and background of a person can also play an important role.

Specific triggers include low self-esteem or body image or boredom, frustration, or loneliness. This type of food has also developed according to a strict diet. If the person's diet contains missing meals or skips certain food groups, binge eating disorder might be triggered.

This isn't Bulimia

Although they can share the very same symptoms, they have different bulimia and binge eating. With bulimia, people eat binge but then start purging the food they consume later. It is achieved by vomiting, diuretics, or laxatives. Binge eaters don't dump their food.

Who at risk?

Everyone may be affected by Binge Eating Disorder regardless of sex, age, or weight. ANAD reports that binge food is now the leading eat disorder among adults in the United States, affecting three to five percent of women (approximately five million) and two percent of men (three million). In contrast to Bulimia or Anorexia, it is a disorder of 'equal opportunities' that affects about the same number of men and women.

Which are the dangers?

Psychological conditions, such as feelings of depression, distress, or anxiety, can require binge eating. People with this disorder feel that they can't control what they eat or what they eat – and only as this consistent over-eating behavior continues.

The evident physical effect of continuous excessive consumption is weight gain – but it does not end there. Obesity is a common effect as two-thirds of people with binge eating are also reported to be obese. The obese and overweight knock effects are, of course, the possible weight-related problems of cardiovascular conditions, hypertension, and type 2 diabetes.

Is it possible to be treated?

Binge eating could be treated successfully. The very first stage is to diagnose it. Usually, a doctor or healthcare professional asks you questions regarding your emotional health, eating habits, how people think and feel regarding food, and the image of your body.

The next move may be a course of self-help or a guided self-help plan (self-help plus a daily appointment with a specialist) or even a specialist clinical intervention for the psychosocial processes of the condition. Cognitive-behavioral therapy (CBT) can also be used to counteract the negative thought habits that can induce binge feeding. Medication could also be administered in some situations.

A healthy, standardized diet plan or weight loss program should be created and implemented in order to address physical issues of weight gain or obesity.

MISTAKES BINGE EATERS MAKE

The mistake which all binge eaters end up making is that you must impose lots of constraints on your food choices to lose weight and stop binge eating.

. . .

We prefer to assume that if we can just consume these things, we can obey these laws forever, or at least until we lose weight, and then all of our issues go away. That's why we're all excited and enthusiastic about our new diet schedule. Generally, your newly discovered plan dictates precisely which food or food groups you can choose and which foods you should keep away. The original instructions make us feel safe and in control because we don't trust ourselves when it comes to food choices. Another person dictates how we have to comply with food, so we are under pressure to make a decision on how to eat; however, the demand for us is to see just how long we can keep to these rules.

Instead, you 'd better follow a food program that allows you to eat any food on the planet so that you never feel deprived of it. Almost all plans limit the groups of foods and drinks to lose some weight on your plan. If for a period of time, you've had to go without a specific form or kind of food, it's unavoidable that you gorge on it. We are still looking for fun as a species. If there is a break between what we are able to eat on a specific plan and what we want to eat that is not on that plan, our inner strength can only last so much before we can understand what our deep desires dictate and that is to give in to prohibited food.

Allowing you to eat every food sounds frightening to the binge eater. It is intuitive to think that all the food we want should be able to eat. We are programmed to believe we need to limit our choices to lose weight. But what we actually have to do is allow us to learn how to incorporate all foods we like into our lives so that they are no longer forbidden and so we don't have to binge on them. It's much easier than you could imagine learning how to moderately enjoy your favorite foods. You can also avoid eating your binge in a single day after doing it.

. . .

This brings me to the second error made by every binge eater, which is to ignore your organism's physical, emotional, and sensory signs.

You have to listen to your digestive system and let it inform you what you want to really eat. As binge eaters, we eat without ever knowing what our bodies are calling for. We don't even know if we want something salty, spicy, juicy, and so on. We may think we 're hungry, but really we are thirsty. We go aimlessly from food to food until we're stuffed, Not quite happy sometimes. The reason is that we didn't stop wondering what we were in the mood. The binge eating process has to become unconscious. It is like there's a force outside you that tells you to eat, that pushes you to eat that which you know would make you fatter and unhealthy.

When you eat what you should want and the foods your body needs are fulfilled much sooner, so you can feel satiated without the need to start the stuffing. It is essential to pause and ask yourself what you really want to eat and do not eat until you know the answer. Believe me, even when you do not see what you want right away, the solution will come to you shortly.

Finally, the third error is to set high expectations that you cannot achieve on a long-term basis.

How often do you begin a diet and pledge that you will not cheat or commit to go to the fitness center and work out an hour five days a week? Before we start, our intentions are fine. But if you are a person who doesn't like to practice what's on earth, would you think you are going to suffer torture on five days a week? It is incongruous and makes us lose if we set ourselves goals or laws that are incompatible with who we are.

. . .

On the other hand, it is a long way to progress in the weight loss plan and the capacity to finish the binge process to focus on less challenging behaviors or to the criteria we set ourselves. For starters, you might be willing to walk 10 minutes a day a few days a week and feel doable for you in the long term. This may not sound like much, and you may start worrying whether it would help to get the weight off quick enough. Nonetheless, it is the little things that can be done quickly (but also easily not done), which make the difference in terms of long-term success.

If we think as well significant, our results appear to be very short. But we do have a higher chance of success when we take a tiny step and remember that we are looking for improvement rather than perfection. Every choice we make may not make a significant difference at this time or that week, but it's just amazing how quickly we sum up these small positive choices and make them lasting success. The key, however, is to select the small steps you would like to take. Then instead of being obliged, you feel encouraged.

What Causes Bulimia?

Bulimia is a genuine emotional wellbeing issue that is brought about by a full scope of organic, mental and social components. Reasons why somebody may be affected by BN can be altogether different, for some individuals for instance nourishment is a method of adapting to troubling feelings or sentiments. Numerous individuals report triggers or negative emotions happening before a gorge as for specific individuals, their dietary problem turns into an approach to manage troublesome emotions and triggers. Confidence has been recorder as a hazard factor for Bulimia as numerous individuals report that they feel useless and have shallow confidence. New research proposes that hereditary qualities such as neurological changes or neuro chemicals in the cerebrum might be factors in creating bulimia.

Psychological social treatment (CBT)

Psychological social treatment (CBT) is the most well-known treatment used for treating bulimia nervosa. CBT can assist you with learning more advantageous perspectives about nourishment and revamp your confidence. CBT might last between 16 and 20 sessions, each enduring about 60 minutes, more than half year term. In the middle of sessions, you will be asked by the advisor to perform various assignments, for example, gradually rolling out little improvements to your dietary patterns, or keeping an everyday journal of when and what you eat.

Examples of Self-improvement

Keeping a journal of your dietary patterns might be useful in understanding what triggers gorges, you may find that care groups are helpful. It very well may be consoling to converse with other people who have had similar emotions and encounters as an expected eight per cent of ladies sooner or later in their lives experience bulimia nervosa.

Dietary patterns help to redress or 'compensate for' nourishment admission practices, including:

- regurgitating
- using intestinal medicines and diuretics
- fasting
- inordinate exercise
- misusing prescriptions to control body weight.

These exercises are not a direction for living, however an indication of a complex emotional wellbeing issue. Consuming fewer calories is the essential hazard factor and trigger all the dietary problems. Individuals with bulimia nervosa frequently have body-weight nearer to the substantial range for their age and stature. It was evaluated that in 2012, more than 78,000 Australian ladies and more than 29,000 men had bulimia nervosa. Individuals with bulimia nervosa frequently take part in practices to shroud the eating, eating fewer carbs, cleansing or exercise.

Physical issues that might be brought about by continuous bulimia nervosa can include:

- sore throat, heartburn, indigestion and indigestion

- stomach and intestinal ulcers
- progressing dental issues because of regurgitating
- ceaseless problems with the gut
- debilitated bones (osteoporosis)
- barrenness in people
- unpredictable heartbeat or a moderate pulse that can inspire cardiovascular breakdown
- electrolyte irregularity from cleansing. This can cause a severe lack of hydration, and harm nerves, muscles and organs.

Manifestations of bulimia nervosa

Understanding the admonition signs and side effects can assist you with recognizing bulimia nervosa early. Early treatment is the ideal approach to start the voyage to a total recuperation.

Physical manifestations of bulimia nervosa

Physical signs and events of bulimia nervosa can include:
- vacillations in body weight
- indications of harm from visit heaving, for example, expanding around the cheeks and jaw, harmed teeth and terrible breath
- visit stoppage, the runs or new nourishment bigotries
- blacking out or unsteadiness that isn't because of another disease or another wellbeing condition
- weakness and failure to rest soundly

In ladies, loss of periods or changed menstrual cycles, even though you can in any case have periods and have bulimia nervosa.

Mental side effects of bulimia nervosa

Psychological signs and side effects of bulimia nervosa can include:
- distraction or fixation on eating, consuming fewer calories, exercise or self-perception
- affectability to remarks about eating, eating less junk food, exercise or self-perception
- sentiments of disgrace, blame and disturbing, particularly in the wake of eating or potentially cleansing
- a mutilated self-perception or outrageous disappointment with body shape -" individuals can think they are fat in any event when they have a sound body weight

- low confidence, sadness, tension or peevishness.

Social side effects of bulimia nervosa

Common signs and side effects of bulimia nervosa can include:

- unexplained vanishing of nourishment stowing away of voraciously consuming food scenes
- undercover conduct around nourishment covering up uneaten nourishment or saying they have eaten when they haven't
- getting increasingly introverted and pulled back
- eating alone and staying away from others at dinner times
- visit excursions to the washroom in the wake of eating
- eating less junk food conduct -" over the top abstaining from excessive food intake, tallying kilojoules, maintaining a strategic distance from specific nutritional categories
- utilization of purgatives, bowel purges, diuretics or craving suppressants
- spending a lot of cash on nourishment
- self-hurting conduct, usage of illicit substances and suicide endeavours.

Analysis of bulimia nervosa

Diagnosing bulimia nervosa can be troublesome for individuals and consequently can go undiscovered for quite a while, it may be discovered following the underlying conditions:

- regularly have bodyweight in the substantial weight territory
- may not show other physical pointers of disease
- may participate in exercises that conceal this psychological maladjustment.

Treatment of Bulimia nervosa

Like other dietary problems, therapy for Bulimia nervosa underlies help for both physical and emotional wellbeing. Early treatment is the ideal approach to help you towards a full recuperation. An experienced support in supporting individuals with a dietary problem is a decent first purpose of contact. When bulimia nervosa is analyzed, your PCP can assist you with collecting a group of medicinal services experts who will be most appropriate to support you. The sorts of social insurance proficient who may be included include:

- a specialist

- a therapist
- a dietitian
- a family advisor
- a social specialist.

How would I start recuperation from a dietary problem?

The inward voices of anorexia and Bulimia murmur that you'll never be content until you get more fit, that your value is estimated by what you look like, etc. In all these murmurs satisfaction and confidence originate from cherishing yourself for who you genuinely are and that is just conceivable with recuperation. The way to occur and rely on a dietary problem begins with conceding you have an issue. This affirmation can be intense, particularly in the case despite everything you're sticking to the conviction even if is sticks to the back of your psyche that weight reduction is the way into your satisfaction, certainty, and achievement.

As anybody can encounter a dietary issue or can show signs of improvement, defeating a nutritional problem is about more than surrendering unfortunate eating practices. It's likewise about adapting better approaches to change to passionate agony and rediscovering who you are past your dietary patterns, weight, and self-perception. Genuine recuperation from a dietary problem includes figuring out how to:

- Tune in to your sentiments.
- Tune in to your body.
- Acknowledge yourself.
- Love yourself.

This may appear to be a ton to handle, however simply recall that you're not the only one. Help is out there, and recuperation is inside your scope. With the right guidance and direction, you can break free from your dietary problem's ruinous example, recapture your wellbeing, and discover the delight in life once more.

Connect for help

When you've chosen to roll out an improvement, opening up about the issue is a significant advance headed straight toward recuperation. It can feel alarming or humiliating to look for help for a dietary problem, so it's imperative to pick somebody who will be steady and really tune in without making a decision about you or dismissing you. This could be a dear companion or relative or a young head, instructor, or school advisor you trust. Or then again, you might be progressively happy with believing in a specialist or specialist. There are no rigid guidelines for informing somebody concerning your dietary issue.

One approach to start by is

"I have something critical to let you know. It's hard for me to discuss this, so it would mean a ton on the off chance that you'd be persistent and listen to me."

You might need to discuss when your dietary problem began, the emotions, musings, and practices included, and how the turmoil has affected you. If you involved another person your companion or relative will have a passionate response to finding out about your dietary problem.

They may feel stunned, vulnerable, confounded, dismal, or even furious. They may not realize how to react or support you. Allow them to process what you're letting them know.

Dietary problem gatherings

While loved ones can be a colossal assistance in offering help, you may likewise need to join a nutritional program. There are numerous sorts of dietary problem bolster gatherings, some are driven by proficient specialists while others are directed via prepared volunteers or individuals who have recuperated from a dietary issue.

You can discover online anorexia and bulimia bolster gatherings, visit rooms, and discussions. These can be especially useful in case you're not prepared to look for the eye to eye help, or you don't have a care group in your general vicinity.

For help finding the below may assist you:
- Approach your primary care physician or advisor for a referral
- Call neighbourhood emergency clinics and colleges
- Call neighbourhood dietary issue focuses and facilities
- Visit your school's advising focus
- Call a helpline recorded in the Get more help area beneath
- Getting treatment for a nutritional problem

While there is a wide range of alternatives accessible for those fighting with nutritional issues, it is imperative to discover the procedure, or a mix of medications, that works best for you.

Compelling treatment should address something other than your side effects and damaging dietary patterns. It ought to likewise address the main drivers of the issue.

Stage 1: Assemble your treatment group

Since dietary issues have genuine, enthusiastic, restorative, and healthful results, it's critical to have a group of experts that can address each part of your concern. To discover a dietary issue treatment in your general vicinity:

- Approach, your essential consideration specialist for a referral
- Check with your neighborhood emergency clinics or restorative focuses
- Ask your school instructor or medical attendant
- Call a helpline recorded in the Resources area beneath

Stage 2: Address medical issues

Dietary issues can be dangerous if you're underweight, your well-being might be in risk, regardless of whether you just vomit or cleanse, so it's essential to get a full restorative assessment.

If the evaluation uncovers medical issues, they should take need. Nothing is a higher priority than your prosperity.

In case you're experiencing any severe problem, you may be hospitalized to guard you.

Stage 3: Make a long haul treatment plan

When medical issues are leveled out your treatment plan may include:

- Individual or gathering treatment. Treatment can assist you in investigating the issues hidden your dietary problem, improve your confidence, and learn reliable methods for reacting to pressure and enthusiastic agony. Various specialists have various techniques, so it is imperative to examine with them your objectives in progressing in the direction of recuperation.

- Family treatment. Family treatment can support you, and your relatives investigate how the dietary issue is influencing your connections and how different relational intricacies might be adding to the topic or blocking recuperation. Together, you'll work to improve correspondence, regard, and backing.

- Nourishing directing. The objective of a nutritionist or dietician is to assist you with fusing smart dieting practices into your regular day to day existence. A nutritionist can change your propensities medium-term, yet over some time, you can figure out how to build up a more advantageous association with nourishment.

- Therapeutic checking. Frequently, treatment will incorporate regular observing by a medicinal specialist to ensure your wellbeing isn't in peril. This may include weekly weigh-ins, blood tests, and other wellbeing screenings.

- Private treatment. In uncommon cases, you may require more help than can be given on an outpatient premise. Individual treatment programs offer round-the-clock care and observing to get you in the groove again. The objective is to get you stable enough to proceed with treatment at home.

Stage 4: Learn self-improvement techniques

While looking for expert assistance is significant, don't disparage your very own purpose in recuperation. The more persuaded you are to comprehend why you built up a dietary problem, and to learn more beneficial adapting aptitudes, the speedier you will see change and recuperating.

How to Deal with binging

How can I, for good, lose weight?

You will lose weight for good by changing your eating habits for good. You will have to eliminate binge eating pressures if you are a binge eater because the extra weight is just a negative side effect of your binge eating. The real concern, therefore, is how to stop binge eating. Let's answer the question one move at a time by breaking it down.

. . .

Why do you get too much to eat?

The response was crystal clear for Beth, one person: job stress. She was always busy and surrounded by friends during the day to eat small amounts of food before she arrived at home at night. Things were going to be tricky during and after dinner.

Like magnets, cookies, or ice cream would become: she couldn't just resist her pull. Her food behavior was an "emotional barometer." When things were on the positive side of her life, her eating was mild. On the other hand, a big binge meant that there was an "emotional earthquake!" With all of the clients, we consider that to be real. In fact, food allows you to change your feeling. It affects your body chemistry literally. Eating is a treat, too. If you feel down, you know that food will change this and even make you feel good. You actually eat more than your body really wants.

How is it so hard to stop eating and feel better?

Second, it works really well! It looks at least like it. Who wants to feel miserable, particularly if you have the power to prevent it? Nutrition is so easy to use in order to face the pressures and difficulties of life, that it is almost irresistibly tempting to use it, even though it becomes clear after a while that the adverse effects are severe and life-threatening.

Secondly, because it is difficult to change habits when you are "unwinding with food" for quite a while, you get significant momentum with food that is hard to break immediately.

And what are the real ways to get rid of binge eating?

1-Focus change: take a hot bath or make a call to a friend. That is, change your focus. If you can enforce them, they will be beneficial, which means that you are really mindful of what you do. But most people lose their ground in great emotional turmoil. They reach an environment where there is no understanding. There is, therefore, no way they can understand and follow the recommendation to change their focus.

2-Consciousness: Thus, it is essential to plan the answer so that you can stay grounded and present and do not enter the Binge Region. How? How? The main word is consciousness. If you know absolutely, you are non-judgmental, which immediately places you right now. Judgment means that you process your life situation intellectually and create positive or negative thoughts and, consequently, positive or negative emotions. That's when you're forced to take action. Let me illustrate that with one client.

She was devastated when Jane came back from her party. She realized very few people seemed to be interested in her and felt like an outsider throughout the night. And then it hit her. She was the room's heaviest woman. This terrible and frightening thought led to an awful feeling of powerlessness, insufficiency, and shame. Shortly after that, Jane hit the 2 pints of ice cream, turned to TV, and entered the binge zone in which she lost track of what she ate ... How did Jane do? It all started with a pessimistic thought, which contributed to a decision: "I'm so overweight that people don't even want to talk with me." That's at the heart of the mental storm of Jane.

Think about situations that cause you to binge to eat. What if you didn't harbor these pessimistic feelings instead? How if you could just move outside your judgment? You still view your life critically, but without marking it correctly or positively, wrongly, or negatively this time. You 'd take the situation as it is. In Jane 's case, being unap-proachable would have been to note what happens, acknowledge it and move on: "I haven't been interacting with many people tonight; oh well, it has been an excellent idea to get out anyway.

But I still hear you "What if I know I missed an important flight or if my employer fires me ...?" The idea remains the same. If things get complicated, it's even more useful. Hold the broader view and take stuff as it is. Why? Does the reality of your situation change? Will the tantrum on everyone's face motivate you to deal best with the situation? This is generally worse. Truth is what it is. What it is. Accepting reality as it stands, rather than telling stories that are simply not true, puts you into the NOW of your life. Taking truth instead of saying things means you are back in charge, living your life.

Being truly conscious will free you from the need to cope. Binge eating involves negating, finding a way to make emotions less intense. When you accept and stand present with what happens in your life, as you face reality as it is, you see that it is not as frightening and fearful as your mind leads you to believe. You would be able to respond more effectively. You 're going to become more grounded and confident.

How are you going to get there? External help will make the process simpler, but you have to know you need no one but you. Tap your inner wisdom, and you will know what is right. The only barrier you can block is yourself. If you are honest in this process, you will succeed. How can I be so confident? Binge eating is about denial. When you are truthful with yourself, you look at the facts and deal with it, rather than looking for ways to deal with it.

AVOIDING BINGE EATING DURING THE HOLIDAYS

We look up to the holidays throughout the year, but why? Some people see this as a family union or a spiritual celebration, but on many days, they drink, eat, shop, and do all things excessively. The more we eat, the emptier we feel.

There are several ways to avoid binge eating and to return to your holidays.

1 Avoid white or black thinking

A characteristic feature of persons with eating disorders is all or nothing-the the extreme view of life and the self without shades of gray.

People with irregular food patterns approach holiday food as an all-or-nothing offer. They eat and limit during the vacation or go to the other extreme and binge, promising to eat after the year."

A safer way is to feed attentively and moderately. We don't feel cheated when we encourage ourselves to enjoy a small portion of our favorite food and then overdo it.

2 Mindful eating practice

When's the last moment you had potatoes mashed? Is dessert food prohibited? Many, especially those with a dietary history, have purchased this unfortunate food phenomenon and have labeled particular food as harmful and others as good.

There seem to be no bad foods. It's just how we are using the menu. If we use food to repel sadness or other emotions or eat to deal with depression, stress, and anxiety, we use food for a purpose that is never meant to be served."

Rather than setting down strict guidelines that mark all foods as excellent or poor, one suggestion is that people consume the food they want when eating it attentively. It may sound like a green light to gorge on fattening foods, but in fact, conscious eating is the opposite of the way other people eat during holidays. It demands that people slow down, take care of the looks and tastes of their meals, and listen carefully to the hunger and satiety of their body.

"When we are eating attentively, we generally eat less because all of our senses are satisfied smell, sight, taste, sound, and touch. It is still possible for us to choose foods for comfort, but we will become much more aware of the emotional connections and taste of these foods. It's fine to eat the strawberry shortcut from Grandma and to remember your relationship with your grandmother as long as you are attentive and enjoy the food, not just your memory."

3 Find Healthy Coping Ways

The holidays will evoke memories and feelings suppressed during the year. Many people are separated from beloveds and from the old days, while others cope with family members with whom they share their holidays. Be aware of their emotions and find safer and more productive ways to cope rather than give in to feelings of food.

Food is not an emotional solution. It's just a brief diversion. Instead of entering the urge with binge, try:

. . .

¥ Take care of how your emotions lead to excessive food.

¥ Have space where you can freely and without fear of criticism or embarrassment share your feelings.

¥ Take time or space to identify what you feel.

¥ Develop an emotional plan in stressful circumstances in advance; for example, if family members comment on your eating habits and weight or force food on you.

4 Don't eat

The break is a socially appropriate time to eat unhealthily. Throughout the days leading up to Christmas and new year's, many people save all their calories. If they sit to feed, they erupt with hunger and cannot be mindful of their intake of food.

Meat is not the only one to blame. The holiday is also a standard period for alcohol consumption, which can keep you from making pure judgments.

Dieting is a binge eating set-up during holidays. It is essential to follow a daily meal plan instead of skipping and overeating.

5 Imbue meaning holidays

It's hard to be Equanimeous on holiday because they've lost their sense, we will bring happiness back to meals and holidays if we can regain a sense of purpose.

. . .

Even if the holidays are about food because you were a teenager, never is enough time for new traditions to show who we are now, not who we were as kids. If it is time to prepare as a family, take a walk every year after dinner, or go to Turkey Trot, having fun in events that do not concentrate on eating can protect against food binge.

6 Get Binge Eating Disorder Support

While holidays can be one of the toughest times to be away from your family and friends, the treatment of eating disorders is also one of the most productive times. You may feel guilty about being punished and not being with your family during the holidays. It is essential to realize that an eating disorder divides you from family members, and despite your physical appearance causes emotional distance. Despite the burden of heightened feelings and complicated family dynamics, the effects of eating disorders frequently escalate during holidays.

A food abuse recovery plan is, in many ways, the perfect place for the holidays, rounded by people who support you, and you will enjoy your holidays at the same time and help you heal.

Many recovery services for eating disorders understand that they are challenging to be on vacation and to make the trip enjoyable by special meals and the use of social events in the community. Such services also benefit and empower families who are allowed to suspend their judgment and accept those who struggle with maintaining healthy body images.

NEUROSCIENTIFIC WAYS TO
UNDERSTAND BULIMIA

Bulimia and the Brain: How Is Neurobiology impacted?
Human BrainBulimia is a serious psychological issue with potential structural organic impacts. As opposed to what is commonly comprehended as a dietary issue, this illness is not simply identified as lack of nourishment or a failure to eat.

Bulimia nervosa is the consequence of a hereditary inclination and could impact psychosocial aspects. Understanding the triggers that lead to bulimia nervosa can help to improve consequent cures and increment the adequacy of current treatments, techniques and conventions that exist for this dietary issue.

Persons who are impacted by bulimia experience very short length timeframes in which a lot of food is consummated, this practice is commonly known as binge eating, unfortunately following this intensive unnatural amount of food the person starts to feel sick and consequently react using medication to induce them poo or make exercise, or a combination of these, to try to stop themselves gaining weight. There is not a specific age for developing this sickness, commonly young women are impacted around the teen ages.

Ongoing Research on Bulimia Nervosa
Ongoing researches showed comparative causes and common personalities that qualify people impacted by this illness. Specialists

have likewise found using mind comparatives that neurological anomalies may be the trigger of bulimia nervosa. A consequence of modified disproportionate serotonin levels may lead to craving, and loss of self-control resulting in bulimia. A patient affected by BN might feel dissatisfaction, this consequence may just not be something that can be switched off and easily resolved.

As the exact cause of BN is not yet known, research states that a mix of unique personality traits, emotions, and thinking patterns, as well as biological and environmental factors might be responsible. Researchers also state that this eating disorder may start with the dissatisfaction of the person's body as well as concerns with the size or shape. It is frequently noted that individuals suffering from bulimia have low self-esteem and fear becoming overweight. The fact that bulimia tends to run in families also suggests that a susceptibility to the disorder might be inherited.

Finding Effective Treatments for Bulimia

The field of neurobiology can be involved in dietary issues, several discoveries in this significant region made by researchers are prompting increasingly successful and improved treatment strategies for bulimia nervosa, which can help improve the patient.

This may incorporate a blend of medicine the board and psychotherapy strategies, which might be useful in lightening indications of bulimia and decreasing inclinations to take part in pigging out then vomiting scenes.

Bulimia Is a Disease

As some common illnesses, for example diabetes, BN impacts by both organic and ecological components, dietary problems are likewise mind-boggling. What's more interesting it that similarly these different sicknesses would be drawn closer and treated comprehensively, bulimia should likewise be overseen in a way that successfully arrives at the hidden causes and the foundations of this illness.

Many factors could impact the development of eating disorders, biology, emotional health, societal expectations, including genetics and other issues. As BN is a dietary issue portrayed by an endless loop of rehashed episodes of troubling pigging out and unseemly endeavours to make up for gorging through retching, extraordinary consuming fewer calories or the abuse of various medications. These side effects are normally determined by an extraordinary distraction with body weight, shape or appearance. After some time these highlights become impulsive and look like those of compulsion.

Bulimia commonly rises in patients not mature yet and is substantially more liable to create in ladies. Studies revealed that 1-2 per cent of ladies have bulimia at some phase in their life. The confusion is related to numerous restorative complexities, and up to 4 per cent of individuals with bulimia accept this disease and flag it as normal.

While existing medications, for example, subjective social treatment (CBT) are compelling for some individuals with bulimia, a significant extent don't improve with talking about treatments. There is a squeezing requirement for new procedures, and specialists are progressively looking towards neuroscience-based innovations that could focus on the hidden neural premise of dietary issues, for example, issues with remuneration preparing or poise.

Following several investigations distributed by the Eating Disorders Research Group at King's University, it has been discovered that dreary transcranial attractive incitement (rTMS effectively and affirmed treatment for wretchedness in the US) was compelling in lessening nourishment desiring in individuals with bulimia. This new investigation inspected the use of transcranial current incitement (tDCS) which is a more affordable and increasingly versatile type of cerebrum incitement that triggers various stimulus to the brain in order to animate explicit pieces of the cerebrum.

For the above examination, 39 individuals got genuine tDCS and fake treatment tDCS, with a time of at any rate 48 hours between the two sessions. The scientists involved in the project used polls when every session to quantify their inclination to voraciously consume food and a scope of other bulimia side effects, including worries about weight and shape, confinement of nourishment admission, levels of poise and confidence.

They found that these bulimia side effects were altogether diminished by the tDCS treatment yet not the fake treatment session. For instance, standard scores on the desire to voraciously consume food scale diminished by 31 per cent following tDCS.

What occurs in the bulimic cerebrum when focused on nourishments

Scientists have realized since the beginning of researches that pressure can assume a key job in bulimia, yet one of the new investigations uncovers how the bulimic mind may see nourishment as a getaway from that pressure. Research states that cerebrums of ladies with bulimia react distinctively to pictures of food, Sarah Fischer, a partner teacher of brain science at George Mason University and a co-creator of the examination, is eager to impart the new research to her customers, she said. -I-™m eager to impart to them that there is conceivably something going on in the cerebrum that makes it progressively hard for them to break this cycle of conduct, instead of feeling self-fault or that 'I need more resolution,' " she said. "I couldn't want anything more than to pursue this examination up to investigate how we can utilize this data to grow all the more organically educated medicines for bulimia."

Her study named -œLady battles bulimia with assistance from cover hounds -œ involved ten ladies with bulimia and ten ladies without dietary problems, prior to the examination, all members were given dinner with a similar measure of supplements in order to avoid feeling hungry, which could slant information. Unbiased and nourishment pictures were shown to the ladies in order to measure which was the trigger of them their entire cerebrums and understand them with the use of an MRI machine. Following the pictures test, ladies were asked to finish an unbiased basic math test. It has been demonstrated that nourishment pictures was still persisting in their cerebrum and was impacting their ability to resolve basic tests. At the end of the test, they were asked to provide some information about their feelings of anxiety and nourishment longings. The MRI machine indicated that ladies with bulimia had diminished bloodstream in a part of the cerebrum called the precuneus while seeing nourishment pictures in the wake of finishing the distressing math issues, though bloodstream fundamentally expanded in that piece of the cerebrum among ladies without bulimia. As the precuneus is related to self-discernment and memory, it has been discovered that less movement in that area among ladies with bulimia was impacted by seeing nourishment pictures.

Despite the fact that the exploration seems fascinating and promising, it falls more into the classification of a pilot study, and the outcomes ought to be seen with an alert, said Dr Guido Frank, a partner educator of psychiatry and neuroscience and partner executive of the dietary problem program at the Un. of Colorado School of Medicine. "The pressure configuration is incredible. We realize that pressure triggers vomiting scenes, and cerebrum imaging can be an exceptionally helpful device," said Frank, who was not associated with the exploration. However "the utilization of pictures is imperfect, as it doesn't disclose to us anything about science in mind," he said of the examination. "The community do not have the foggiest idea what causes bulimia nervosa; notwithstanding, the rehashed scenes of pigging out and cleansing, self-instigated spewing, cause enormous changes in mind synthetic substances."

The pervious examination was replicated including 26 ladies with a background marked by Bulimia and 22 ladies with no dietary issues, who had their minds filtered in MRI machines. At the same time, they were given sugar water either in the wake of fasting for 16 hours or after having a morning meal of bagels and cream cheddar. The specialists at that point examined the cerebrum pictures to decide contrasts in how the ladies reacted to the water's sweet taste when hungry or full. The analysts found that the minds of ladies with no history of Bulimia indicated altogether more significant action in the left putamen and amygdala when they were given sugar water after fasting, versus after they were nourished.

Those pieces of the celebrum are related with assessing rewards, for example, how compensating a taste is. Concerning the ladies with a past filled with Bulimia, there was no such contrast, and their left amygdalae had more noteworthy action when nourishments contrasted, which may hold pieces of information to the gorging parts of Bulimia. Ely, who was associated with the examination while at the University of California, San Diego, compared the discoveries to shopping for food said: "On the off chance that you go shopping for food when you're eager, you're bound to discover everything look fulfilling. We will work in general purchase all the more profoundly tasteful nourishments," then continued "On the off chance that you go shopping for food when you're full, you're not as intrigued, and you'll adhere to your basic food item list. You don't get pulled and inspired in a major manner by a prize," she said. "Somebody with bulimia, when their minds go to the allegorical market when they're full, regardless they're attracted to a sweet taste, although they're full." Restrictions of the examination incorporate its small example size, because of the significant expense of cerebrum imaging, and the way that the entirety of the members with a past filled with Bulimia was recouped or transmitted from the turmoil, Ely said. "It would be significant for us to test to check whether this distinction because of taste existed or how it may introduce itself in somebody who presently has bulimia," she said. Moreover, "we took a gander at the sweet taste, and we realize that exceptionally unmistakable nourishments come in numerous structures, for example, high-fat sorts, as well. In any case, nobody knows whether Bulimia causes such changes in the cerebrum or whether such contrasts in mind are related with vulnerability to Bulimia, Ely said.

Dr Walter Kaye, who drove the investigation, trusts that that question could be replied as more research is directed explicitly on the cerebrums of bulimics later on. "We truly don't comprehend why individuals pig out then vomit. Stress and negative mindset states are identified with this concept. There's been this inquiry concerning whether individuals limit and get ravenous and gorge, or whether they can't close off eating once they begin to eat," said Kaye, an educator and author and executive of the dietary issues program at the University of California, San Diego. "I need to let you know, human conduct is confounded enough that there might be more than one reason," he said.

As specialists keep on scanning for a reason, Fitzgibbons, the Eating Recovery Center envoy in Denver, accentuated that recuperating is no puzzle. "Regardless of how miserable life appears, there is expectation and life on the opposite side of a dietary issue," she said. "Give recuperation a genuine and legitimate exertion. It's anything but a straight voyage, so give yourself some beauty and pardoning simultaneously. ... Life shows signs of improvement. Ensure you're there to see it."

Bulimia nervosa is a sort of dietary problem that influences 1-3% of people, BN is a genuine nutritional problem where somebody may feel that they have lost authority over their eating and assess themselves as indicated by their body shape and weight. Somebody with Bulimia may feel trapped in a cycle of eating enormous amounts of nourishment (known as 'gorging'), and afterwards captivating with practices to make up for this as an endeavour to avert putting on weight (known as purging).

HELPFUL 10 TIPS TO OVERCOME BINGE EATING

Voraciously consuming food technically known as BED is viewed as the most widely recognized dietary problem in the United States. BED is about more than nourishment, individuals who are determined to have BED experience particular scenes of eating such as extreme stomach extensions, standard gorge scenes can prompt to weight gain that consequently can lead to conditions like diabetes and coronary illness.

Most of BED patients feel ashamed of what they feel doing and worry that others will find out. As a result, some of the symptoms of the condition are beneficial.

There are several warning signs of BED:
- Fast gain in weight or obesity
- Continuous changes in weight
- Frequent intake of excessive food quantities in a short period, typically less than two hours;
- No strategies for the removal of food
- Eating easily, swallowing sometimes without chewing
- Feeling a lack of control over your food
- Alone to eat
- Secret eating practices
- Hide or conceal food, usually high calorie / "junk" food

- Early in the night to eat
- Consuming huge amounts of food without hunger
- Contempt and guilt for self after unnecessary consumption
- Tackling emotional and/or behavioral problems such as pain, unhappiness or consuming frustration
- Consuming food to the point that it is unpleasant or sometimes painful
- Attributing successes and weight defeats

Avoiding social circumstances, in particular food circumstances

Luckily, there are a lot of techniques you can attempt " both at home and with the assistance of an expert " to lessen scenes of voraciously consuming food. Here are 15 hints to help beat voraciously consuming food.

BED patients also say that their binge food is something they find illegal or unsafe. For instance, one patient described eating large quantities of bread, sweets, and pastries secretly because of medical obesity that was restricted from her daily diet. "The worst, the better"

As we begin to explore various forms of self-control, BED is related to a number of deficits. Persons with BED tend to do worse with tasks related to engine inhibition and attention, and these shortfalls appear to be associated with the severity of binge eating rather than obesity.

There are many empirically validated treatment strategies for BED that share the goal of reducing binge episodes and the psychopathology involved. The Gold standard is cognitive behavior therapy (CBT), which focuses on maladaptive eating habits by means of a combination of eating patterns, self-monitoring, and behavioral and cognitive management skills. The cognitive approaches include the recognition and modification of cognitive biases that lead to binge eating behavior. Since binge eating is commonly used as a way to regulate negative feelings, some therapies have the emotional control on patients.

You 're over-eating because of stress, annoyance, anger, unhappiness, or boredom? Is it a nasty habit that you soon won't seem to break over food?

1. Discard the eating regimen

Craze diets can frequently be undesirable, and studies show that excessively prohibitive eating techniques may trigger scenes of overeating. For instance, one investigation in 496 immature young ladies found that fasting was related with a greater danger of overeating, another research in 103 ladies saw that avoiding certain nourishments brought about expanded yearnings and more risk of indulging.

Rather than following eating regimens that attention on removing whole nutritional categories or fundamentally cutting calorie admission to get more fit rapidly focus on eating all the more entire natural nourishments, for example, organic products, vegetables, and whole grains, and moderate your admission of treats as opposed to barring them. This can help diminish overeating and advance better wellbeing.

Studies show that fasting or disposing of specific nourishments from your eating routine might be related with expanded yearnings and gorging. Concentrate on eating healthy nourishments as opposed to abstaining from excessive food intake or removing certain nourishments.

2. Abstain from skipping suppers

Setting a regular eating calendar and adhering to it is one of the best approaches to defeat gorging. Skipping suppers can add to desires and increment the danger of indulging.

Study indicate that eating one enormous supper every day expanded degrees of glucose and the craving stimulating hormone called ghrelin to a more remarkable degree than eating three meals a day.

Another examination in 38 individuals found that sticking to a regular eating schedule was related with a diminished recurrence of overeating. A calendar eating plan is the best solution to overcome skipping supers, switching to a common eating example can decrease the danger of indulging and might be related to lower levels of ghrelin and fasting glucose.

3. Practice care-

Care is a training that includes tuning in to your body and focusing on how you feel right now. This strategy can avoid gorging by helping an individual figure out how to perceive when they never again feel hungry. An investigation on 14 patients found that rehearsing care contemplation diminished the occurrence of voraciously consuming food and enthusiastic eating. Another little examination indicated that joining care with intellectual, social treatment may improve eating conduct and mindfulness.

Have a go at turning the attention in to your body and perceive when yearning decreases. Moreover, attempt to eat gradually and appreciate nourishment to advance smart dieting practices. Rehearsing care can enable you to perceive when you're never again ravenous, which can improve your eating practices and lessen the frequency of overeating.

4. Remain hydrated

Drinking a lot of water for the day is a basic yet powerful approach to control yearnings and quit indulging, it may sound a light approach bu studies show that expanding water admission could be connected to diminished appetite and calorie consumption.

For instance, one examination in 24 more established grown-ups found that drinking 17 ounces (500 ml) of water before eating a supper diminished the number of calories devoured by 13%, another investigation in more seasoned grown-ups demonstrated that drinking 13 to 17 ounces (375--"500 ml) of water 30 minutes before a dinner altogether diminished craving and calorie consumption while expanding sentiments of satiety during the day (9Trusted Source).-

Different investigations demonstrate that drinking more water can help digestion and weight reduction. The measure of water every individual should drink day by day relies upon various elements, it's ideal for tuning in to your body and drink when you feel parched to guarantee you're remaining very much hydrated. Drinking more water can keep you feeling full and anticipate voraciously consuming food.

5. Attempt yoga

Yoga is training that joins both the body and psyche by using specific breathing activities, stances, and reflection to decrease pressure and improve unwinding. Studies demonstrate that yoga can help empower good dieting propensities and lessen the danger of emotional eating.

An investigation found that 50 individuals with BED indicated that rehearsing yoga for 12 weeks prompted a considerable decrease in gorging, another examination in 20 young ladies found that joining yoga with outpatient dietary problem treatment diminished sadness, nervousness, and self-perception unsettling influences which could all be factors engaged with passionate eating.

Researches additionally shows that yoga can diminish levels of pressure hormones like cortisol to monitor pressure and avert voraciously consuming food. A good attempt might be joining a nearby yoga studio to begin adding this sort of activity to your everyday practice. You can likewise use online video classes or recordings to exercise at home in order to reach inner peace and fight gorging stimulus.

6. Eat more fibre-

Fibre moves gradually through your stomach related tract, keeping you feeling full more. Some examination proposes that expanding fibre admission could cut longings, diminish hunger, and nourishment consumption. A investigation lasted 2-week found that enhancing twice a day with fibre found in vegetables diminished yearning and calorie admission.

A consequent study found that in 10 grown-ups taking 16 grams of prebiotic fibre every day developed degrees of explicit hormones that impact satiety and virtually diminished sentiments of yearning. Organic products, vegetables, and entire grains are only a couple of fibre-rich nourishments that can keep you feeling full that can help keep you feeling full of diminishing calorie admission and sentiments of craving.

7. Wipe out the kitchen

Having loads of junk food in the kitchen may trigger voraciously consume, keeping solid nourishments close by can lessen your danger of emotional eating by constraining the number of undesirable choices.

Start by getting out handled nibble nourishments like chips, cakes, and pre-bundled food sources and swapping them for more beneficial other options. Embedding your kitchen with natural products such as vegetables, protein-rich nourishments, entire grains, nuts, and seeds can improve your eating regimen and diminish your danger of voraciously consuming food.

Getting rid of nourishments from your kitchen and loading up reliable options can improve diet quality and make it harder to consume food voraciously.

8. Start hitting the Centre

Studies show that adding activity to your routine could anticipate and lower voraciously consuming food, for instance, a 6-month study on 77 individuals demonstrated that expanding week after week practice recurrence halted voraciously consuming food in 81% of members. Another examination in 84 ladies found that matching intellectual, social treatment with customary exercise was fundamentally increasingly compelling at diminishing the recurrence of voraciously consuming food than Medication alone.

A consequent research, based on the previous examinations recommends that activity can diminish feelings of anxiety and improve the state of mindfulness to forestall enthusiastic eating.

Strolling, running, swimming, biking, and playing sports are only a couple of various types of physical activities that can help alleviate pressure and lessen voraciously consuming food. Studies show that practicing them can lessen the danger of voraciously consuming food and decline feelings of anxiety.

9. Have breakfast each day

Beginning every vacation day with a healthy breakfast may lessen the danger of voraciously consuming food later in the day.

A few examinations have discovered that keeping up a standard eating design is related to less voraciously consuming food and lower levels of ghrelin. This hormone as previously stated stimulates the sentiments of craving and additionally, topping off on the correct nourishments can keep you feeling full to control yearnings and lessen hunger for the day.

An investigation on 15 individuals found that having a high-protein breakfast diminished the amount of ghrelin released in the blood to a more remarkable degree than having a high carb breakfast.

Eating fibre-and protein-rich oats appeared to improve hunger control and advance totality in another examination in 48 individuals.

In addition to the tip stated previously, complete your breakfast of fibre-rich nourishments, for example, natural products, vegetables, or entire grains, with a decent wellspring of protein to abstain from gorging. Eating a fibre-and protein-rich breakfast can avert yearnings and keep you fulfilled for the duration of the morning.

10. Get enough rest-

Rest influences your craving levels and hunger as lack of sleep might be connected to gorging. An investigation on 146 individuals found that those with BED announced fundamentally a more significant number of manifestations of sleep deprivation than individuals without a past filled with this condition.

Another examination demonstrated that shorter rest length was related with more significant levels of the yearning hormone ghrelin and lower levels of leptin --" the hormone answerable for advancing completion.

OVERCOMING BINGING

Locate the Best Binge Eating Treatment Programs and Dual Diagnosis Rehabs

It is critical to recognize voraciously consuming food issue from other dietary problems, many patients affected by bulimia manifesting gorging may show overeating confusion regularly. Individuals who gorge regret the action itself and even disgust after their gorges, frequently this post-gorge wretchedness prompts one more gorge, dovetailing into a winding of impulsive eating and disgrace.

The eventual outcomes of gorging show in both physical and mental side effects that individuals who overeat may get discouraged, wracked with blame and loaded up with self-hatred for their practices.

Overabundance weight and ruinous dietary decisions may bring corpulence issues such as coronary illness, hypertension, elevated cholesterol, diabetes and musculoskeletal issues. The double effect on the brain and body makes overeating particularly hard to conquer alone.

Voraciously consuming food is likewise not quite the same as nourishment fixation and may convey to physiological reliance on explicit nourishments, though overeating is progressively aimless.

Potential Causes

Like other dysfunctional behaviors, there is certifiably not a solitary cause for a gorging issue since the human cerebrum and its feelings are so unpredictable. As indicated in the National Eating Disorders Association (NEDA), roughly 1 to 5% of the population has voraciously consumed food issue, so there is a decent possibility that you know or have known somebody with it in your group of friends.

Numerous individuals who voraciously consume food feel detached, additionally notwithstanding mainstream thinking, BED influences the two sexual orientations, while ladies have a somewhat higher inclination to gorge, NEDA likewise reports that 40% of the individuals who overeat are men. Statistics report that men are frequently the last to look for help and go out on a limb of treatment or backing.

Which Treatment Is Right for You?

When you have made the first and regularly the most troublesome advance of looking for help for voraciously consuming food, the question for the best treatment alternative starts with the following question:

Which office is the best indicated for me?

What is remedial the best methodology that can decrease my pain?

Nowadays treatment alternatives are able to suit all characters, foundations and timetables. Various alternatives may be as follows:

Double Diagnosis Therapy

Many gorge eaters go into treatment accepting food disorders as their single issue yet finding that they experience the ill effects of other emotional wellness issues, for example, clinical melancholy or bipolar aspect. As indicated by the US National Health Service, it is assessed that half of individuals who are recognized as gorge eaters experience the ill effects of clinical discouragement.

Treating both the eating and the psychological issue pair enables patients to increase significant self-information about their inclinations and triggers. Some defeat their fundamental analysis through talk treatment alone, and others with the progressively serious issue have alluded to a specialist for the professionally prescribed drug.

Professionally prescribed Medication

Contingent to these finding, various drugs may enable the individuals and lead to the condition of gorge eater. Particular serotonin inhibitors (SSRIs) help reduce the burdensome and mitigate the effect of emotions. While these are not recommended continuously notwithstanding talk treatment, numerous individuals with overeating confusion find that medication same time as treatments. All the previously mentioned choices might be embraced on an outpatient premise; in any case, it might be progressively compelling to enter an inpatient private dietary program office for treatment.

Gathering Support and Self-Help

Self-improvement and gathering support are new pathways to long haul achievement. Overeating turmoil (BED) is a sort of bolstering and dietary problem that is presently perceived as formal analysis. It influences nearly 2% of individuals worldwide and can cause further medical issues connected to loss of weight, for example, elevated cholesterol levels and diabetes.

Dietary problems are not about nourishment alone, which is the reason they're perceived as a mental issue, as individuals usually create them as a method for managing a more profound effect or another psychiatric condition, for example, tension or gloom.

What is voraciously consuming food issue, and what are the side effects?-

Individuals with BED may eat an out of normal amount of food in a short length of time, regardless of whether they aren't eager to consume. An individual may feel a discharge or help necessity during a gorge and experience sentiments of disgrace or loss of control a while later, the side effects of the practice may be:

- eating substantially more quickly than typical
- eating until awkwardly full
- eating enormous amounts without feeling hungry
- eating alone because of sentiments of humiliation and disgrace
- emotions of blame or disturb with oneself

Individuals with BED regularly experience feelings of extreme sadness and misery about their gorging, body shape, and weight.

BED is described by rehashed scenes of open admission of surprisingly a lot of nourishment in a brief timeframe. These scenes are joined by sentiments of blame, disgrace, and mental trouble.

What causes voraciously consuming food issue?

The reasons for BED are not surely known yet likely because of an assortment of hazard factors, including:

- Hereditary qualities. Individuals with BED may have expanded affect-ability to dopamine, a concoction in the cerebrum that is explicable with regards to the sentiment of remuneration and delight

- Gender. BED is more typical in ladies than in men, in the United States, 3.6% of ladies experience BED sooner or later in their lives, contrasted and 2.0% of men, this might be because of fundamental organic elements Source

- Changes in the cerebrum. There are signs that individuals with BED may have differences in cerebrum structure that outcome in an uplifted reaction to nourishment and less poise).

- Body size. Half of the individuals with BED have heftiness and 25 per cent of this half are looking for weight reduction

- Self-perception. Individuals with BED frequently have a negative self-perception. Body disappointment, abstaining from excessive food intake and gorging add to the improvement of the turmoil

- Overeating. Those influenced frequently report a past filled with gorging as the primary indication of the chaos, this incorporates overeating in adolescence and the high school years.

- Self injury. Upsetting life occasions, for example, misuse, demise, detachment from a relative, or a fender bender, are hazard factors. Youth harassing because of weight may likewise contribute.

- Other mental conditions. Practically 80% of individuals with BED have at any rate one other psychological issue, for example, fears, gloom, post-awful pressure issue (PTSD), bipolar issue, uneasiness, or substance misuse.

A scene of overeating can be activated by pressure, abstaining from excessive food intake, negative emotions identifying with body-weight or body shape, the accessibility of nourishment, or fatigue.

The reasons for BED are not entirely known. Similarly, as with other dietary issues, an assortment of hereditary, ecological, social, and mental dangers are related to its improvement.

How is BED analyzed?

While a few people may at times gorge, for example, at Thanksgiving or any other occasion with excess of food, it doesn't mean they have BED, despite having encountered a portion of the side effects recorded previously.

BED commonly begins in the late teenagers to mid-twenties, even though it can happen at any age. Individuals, for the most part, need backing to help defeat BED and build up a sound association with nourishment. Whenever left untreated, BED can keep going for a long time.

What are the wellbeing dangers?

BED is related with a few substantial physical, emotional, and social wellbeing dangers.

Up to half of the individuals with BED have weight problems, corpulence expands the danger of coronary illness, stroke, type 2 diabetes, and malignant growth.

Notwithstanding, a few investigations have discovered that individuals with BED have considerably more danger of building up these medical issues and individuals with the heftiness of a similar weight who don't have BED.

Other wellbeing dangers related to BED incorporate other concerning issues like ceaseless agony conditions, asthma, and bad-tempered gut disorder (IBS).-

In ladies, the condition is related to a danger that may lead to pregnancy impossibility, and the improvement of polycystic ovary disorder (PCOS)

In addition to the above, research has indicated that individuals with BED report difficulties with social collaborations, contrasted and individuals without the condition.

Furthermore, individuals with BED have a high pace of hospitalization, outpatient care, and crisis division visits, contrasted and the individuals who don't have a nourishing or dietary issue. Even though these wellbeing dangers are noteworthy, there are various viable medicines for BED.

BED is connected to an expanded danger of weight addition and heftiness, just as related maladies like diabetes and coronary illness.

There are additionally other wellbeing dangers, including rest issues, eternal torment, psychological wellness issues, and decreased personal satisfaction.-

What are the treatment choices?

The treatment plan for BED relies upon the causes and seriousness of the dietary issue, just as individual objectives.

Treatment may target voracious consuming food practices, over-abundance weight, self-perception, emotional wellness issues, or a blend of these. Treatment choices incorporate intellectual conduct treatment, relational psychotherapy, rationalistic conduct treatment, weight reduction treatment, and prescription. These might be completed on a balanced premise, in a gathering setting, or a self-improvement group.-

In specific individuals, only one kind of treatment might be required, while others may need to attempt various mixes until they locate the correct fit.

A therapeutic or emotional wellness expert can give counsel on choosing an individual treatment plan.

Subjective social treatment

Subjective social treatment (CBT) for BED centers around breaking down the connections between negative musings, senti-ments, and practices identified with eating, body shape, and weight.

When the reasons for pessimistic feelings and examples have been recognized, systems can be created to assist individuals with evolving them. Explicit mediations incorporate defining objectives, self-observing, accomplishing standard dinner designs, changing musings about self and weight, and empowering solid weight-control propensities.

One investigation found that after 20 sessions of CBT, 79% of members were never again voraciously consuming food, with 59% of them still following one year.

On the other hand, guided self-improvement CBT is another alter-native. In this arrangement, members are typically given a manual to work through without anyone else, alongside the chance to go to some extra gatherings with a specialist to help direct them and set objectives.

The self-improvement type of treatment is frequently less expensive and progressively available, and there are sites and versatile applications that offer help.

Self-improvement CBT has been demonstrated to be a powerful option in contrast to customary CBT (24, 25Trusted Source). CBT centres around distinguishing the negative emotions and practices that reason voraciously consuming food and helps set up procedures to improve them. It is the best treatment for BED and might be finished with an advisor or in a self-improvement position.

Relational psychotherapy
Relational psychotherapy (IPT) depends on the possibility that voraciously consuming food is a way of dealing with stress for uncertain individual issues, for example, melancholy, relationship clashes, substantial life changes, or hidden social problems. The objective is to distinguish the particular issue connected to the eating conduct, recognize it, and afterwards roll out necessary improvements more than 12 four months. Treatment may either be in a gathering design or on a coordinated premise with a prepared advisor, and it might now and then be joined with CBT.

16 Ways To Overcome Binge Eating Disorder
Overeating confusion can be a troublesome issue to fight as one may require the help of a dietary treatment, this issue might be particularly disturbing because of the way that nourishment a radicate issue. How at that point would you be able to defeat this issue related to voraciously consuming food issue?

- Tell somebody. Regardless of whether just a single individual thinks about your issue, in any event, you will never again be separated from everyone else in your battle.

- Search out treatment and treatment. Try out a dietary issue treatment office or go to the treatment session. Be happy to learn

- Convey constrained measures of nourishment at home. Even though this might be all the more a problem, it will restrict allurements at home.

- Unwind. Put aside time to appreciate life and participate in a fun movement.

- Pardon yourself. You can't change the past. You can just gain from your mix-ups.

- Exercise. Plan out a proper exercise program you will want to keep up.

- Decide the causes and triggers of your issue. By doing this, you would then be able to find a way to forestall further gorges.-

- Have breakfast day by day. The individuals who don't consistently have breakfast are progressively inclined to gorging and eating fatty dinners later in the day.

- Offer your interests with loved ones. Never confine yourself.

- Take sufficient supplements. On the off chance that you don't expend enough supplements for your body, think about taking nutrient and mineral enhancements.

- Get self-improvement guides. These books will energize you and regularly offer accommodating guidance, particularly if they are fixated on overeating.

- Go to a care group. Realizing that others fight with similar issues may soothe pressure.

- Chat with a nutritionist. The individual can assist you in setting up a fitting dinner plan.

- Write in a diary. This may help, particularly when you incline to consume food voraciously.

- Try not to consume fewer calories. Prevailing fashion eats less once in a while help for significant periods, and extremely severe eating regimen plans may just aggravate your issue.

- Love yourself for what your identity is, not what you resemble.

CONCLUSION

Acknowledge the fact that bulimia nervosa is part of your daily life is the perfect method for starting the fight against it, for instance, you will be able to know how your body works and how to overcome this illness.

There will be no harmful chemicals involved and it will actually be you that have grown them. Feeling proud for being able to fight your own illness either for consumption or profession is one of the most useful benefits of such systems. Having a plan when it comes to methods is important because success always starts with a solid plan.

Planning means that you have researched and found out the necessary information about the illness you wish to cure such nutritional needs or your body needs. You will plan for the necessary supplies you will need and the necessary equipment of your system that should be chosen based on what you have to offer.

Do you have to offer enough space, work, effort, determination, and time? Based on your answers, you can choose the best system to suit your answers. Having a week by week schedule will help you immensely and you should include all the maintenance requirements of your system as well as the care of your body and mind.